Where's Alice?
Welcome to Girlguiding UK's fab Centenary celebrations at Harewood House! Hidden in this picture somewhere is Brownie Alice. Can you spot her?

FuSion
A Spectacular Way to Celebrate our Centenary!

face painting

NATURE DISCOVERY

Can you spot h...

Contents

BE SAFE

You should be able to have a go at everything in your Brownie Annual, but sometimes it is a good idea to get some help. When you see this symbol, ask an adult if they can lend a hand.

Be safe

Badge link

Friend to animals

BADGES!

Look out for this 'Badge link' sign. If you enjoyed something in this Annual you might like to work towards the badge shown too!

Girlguiding UK
girls in the lead

© The Guide Association 2009

Published by Girlguiding UK
17–19 Buckingham Palace Road
London SW1W 0PT
www.girlguiding.org.uk

Girlguiding UK is an operating name of The Guide Association. Registered charity number 306016. Incorporated by Royal Charter.

Girlguiding UK Trading Service ordering code 6005
ISBN 978 0 85260 246 1

All Brownie and Guide photographs © The Guide Association.
Cover photograph by Laura Ashman.
Internal photographs by Laura Ashman and Anne-Marie Briscombe.
Other photographs courtesy of Shutterstock unless otherwise stated.

Girlguiding UK would like to thank all the Brownies and their Leaders who took part in the development and production of this resource.

Project Coordinator: Helen Channa
Written by Kaisu Fagan, Kimberly Haddrell, Verity Hancock, Emma Joyce, Mariano Kälfors, Kate Knighton, Abigail Latter, Harriet Lowe, Helen Mortimer, Hannah Rainford

Project Editor: Mariano Kälfors
Picture Editor: Abigail Latter
Designers: Helen Davis, Angie Daniel, Kimberly Haddrell, Ana Salgado, Yuan Zhang
Cover design: Kimberly Haddrell
Production: Les Girling, Wendy Reynolds
Printed by Pindar

Readers are reminded that during the lifespan of this publication there may be changes to Girlguiding UK's policy, or legal requirements, that may affect the accuracy of information contained within these pages.

FSC Mixed Sources
Product group from well-managed forests and other controlled sources
www.fsc.org Cert no. CU-COC-808383
© 1996 Forest Stewardship Council

Brownie top 10

1. FUN!
Brownies have all kinds of fun – games fun, adventure fun, holiday fun and lots, lots more!

3. BADGES!
Lots and lots of Brownie badges to do! My favourite ones are: wild Life

exsp Lorer

4. MY PACK
Georgina Hannah
Holly P
Katie
Holly Smith
Lilly
Nahtsha B
Nantsha Lilly

7. MY BROWNIE LEADERS
Brown owl
flky owl
snowy owl

8. MY...(ADD YOUR OWN FAVOURITE BROWNIE THING HERE)
The Birthday Song My Birthday June the 21th

9. (AND HERE)

2. THE BROWNIE PROMISE

We make a special Promise like thousands of other Brownies all over the world. Ours is:

I promise that I will do my best:
To love my God
To serve the Queen and my country,
To help other people
And
To keep the Brownie Guide Law.

The Brownie Guide Law is:

A Brownie Guide thinks of others before herself and does a Good Turn every day.

5. MY SIX

Hannah
my zer
Holy O

6. MY BEST BROWNIE FRIENDS

Georgina
Katie
Molly O
Holly Shi
Lilly

10. (AND HERE!)

arean sorlos

Nantasha Lilly
Nantasha Botton
Hannah

Ways to celebrate

It's the year 2010 and the guiding Centenary is now here! Do you know what that means? Celebrations!!!

★ GUIDING ★ CELEBRATES ★

It's 100 years since guiding began! It's a very big number, a very big birthday, and therefore a very big celebration! All around the UK, guiding units will be making sure that our 100th birthday will be lots of fun and will go off with a very big bang right through the year!

★ BROWNIES ★ CELEBRATE ★

As Brownies are the largest section (with 250,000 members and counting), no guiding celebrations would be complete without Brownies taking part in the fun! During 2010 there will be lots of events just for Brownies!

★ THE ★ BIG ★ BROWNIE ★ TAKEOVER ★

Adventures all over the UK and Europe for Brownies are called *The Big Brownie Takeover*. Why? Because we're taking over! We're taking over at camps, at outdoor activity centres (TACs), at ICANDO, at theme parks, at woodlands, at winter wonderlands, at carnivals, at Alice's Wonderland, at the seaside, on steam trains and lots, lots more!!!

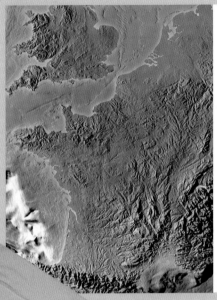

★ BROWNIES ★ TAKEOVER ★ EUROPE

On one particular Takeover Adventure, Brownies and their Leaders will have the chance to celebrate our Centenary in a theme park in Belgium! Brownies from all over the UK will gather at Popsland theme park in Belgium for an Adventure with a truly continental flavour.
Who knows, it could be you!

Badge link

Craft

Want to find out more about the guiding Centenary in general? Read pages 10–13 and 66–67.

★ BROWNIES ★ TAKEOVER ★ THE OUTDOORS

Brownies will also have the chance to visit some of the finest outdoor activity centres around the UK! You can choose from Shropshire, Surrey, Devon, Perthshire, Dorset, Lincolnshire, the Brecon Beacons – and even France!

★ TAKEOVER ★ EVERYWHERE

Put simply, Brownie Takeovers are happening everywhere, and your Brownie Leader will be able to tell you all about it. You can even create your very own Brownie Takeover, so get planning with your unit now!

9

SUPER BROWNIE TIME TRAVELLER

Illustrated by Toni Goffe

Party-planning countdown

Our Centenary is a great excuse for a party! Here's how to organise the perfect bash.

★ ONE ★ MONTH ★ BEFORE...

What's the occasion for the party? Where are you going to have it? At your house? At a hall? At the swimming pool? At the local bowling alley? Start by talking to whoever is going to pay for your party.

Think about a date and time for your party. Weekends are always best and if it's your birthday, choose the weekend nearest your special day.

Create a guest list. Have a mix of school and Brownie friends. It doesn't matter if not everyone knows each other. Parties are a great way to make new friends.

Badge link

Hostess

COME TO OUR PARTY

★ THREE ★ WEEKS ★ BEFORE...

Be unique and create your own beautiful party invitations. Find out how to make your own fab party invitations on page

★ TWO ★ WEEKS ★ BEFORE...

Decide on a theme for your party. It can be something as simple as having pink and blue balloons or as complicated as fancy dress. The choice is yours.

Have some party games set up. You may not use them, but they are on hand if your guests start getting bored.

★ ONE ★ WEEK ★ BEFORE...

Make sure you've got your outfit sorted. If you can't afford a brand new outfit, get your friends round and see if you can swap clothes for the day. While you're there, you could try experimenting with some funky new hairstyles. Check out the Brownies website for some hairstyle tips! www.girlguiding.org.uk/brownies

Music is guaranteed to get the party started. If you don't have a lot of your own tunes, ask your friends to bring their own. For the latest chart tunes, listen to a radio station or a music channel on TV.

★ THREE ★ DAYS ★ BEFORE...

Decide what food to provide. We've got some yummy party recipes on page 20. Ask your friends what food they like, and make sure you know about any allergies (like nuts, milk, etc).

★ ON ★ THE ★ DAY...

Get glammed up and ready to party!
Make sure you have a great time – remember it's your special day!

Party essentials

Everything you need for a proper celebration!

You will need

You will need

- balloons
- confetti, scraps of paper, glitter

★ CONFETTI ★ BALLOONS

1. Put some confetti, scraps of paper or glitter into the unfilled balloon.
2. Blow the balloon up. Make sure you don't breathe in through your mouth or you'll end up with a mouthful of confetti and glitter!
3. Tie off the balloon. Wow! You've created some very glamorous confetti balloons.

★ PARTY ★ INVITATIONS

For creative party invitations, take a look at the Activities section of the Brownies website. There are some printable invitations for you to colour in. If you are feeling a bit more adventurous, you can also try making your own card!

- a blown up balloon
- old newspapers, torn into strips
- PVA glue
- scissors
- sticky tape
- string
- sweets and small prizes
- apron or old clothes to wear

★ PIÑATA!

Warning! This activity can get very messy!

1 Cover the newspaper strips in glue and stick them over the balloon. Leave it overnight to dry.

2 Repeat step 1 again.

3 Using the scissors, carefully cut out a hole in the top (do not throw the cut-out away!)

4 Pop the balloon if it hasn't already. Make two small holes either side of the top hole and thread string through for hanging it up.

5 Decorate the paper shape. Try tissue paper, foil, buttons, paint... the more colourful the better!

6 Fill the piñata (pronounced *pin-yaa-ta*) with sweets and small goodies and use sticky tape to fix the top back over the hole.

At your party, take it in turns with your friends to hit the piñata to try and release the prizes. Be gentle, and don't hit any of your friends!

Be safe

Brownies

Artist

Craft

Badge link

19

Party favourites

These recipes are perfect to share with friends at any party!

★ CENTENARY ★ MILKSHAKES ★

INGREDIENTS

Banana milkshake
- ★ 1 banana (peeled)
- ★ 150g vanilla ice cream
- ★ 250ml skimmed milk

Strawberry milkshake
- ★ 5 large strawberries
- ★ 150g strawberry ice cream
- ★ 250ml skimmed milk

Blueberry milkshake
- ★ 75g fresh or frozen blueberries
- ★ 150g vanilla ice cream
- ★ 250ml skimmed milk

Be safe

YOU WILL NEED

- ★ a food blender
- ★ tall glasses
- ★ decorations – bendy straws, paper umbrellas, swizzle sticks!

Badge link

Cook · Cook

I. Pick your choice of fruit and carefully chop into slices (the blueberries can be kept whole).

2. Place the fruit, ice cream and milk in a food blender and whizz for around 30 seconds to a minute until smooth.

3. Pour your milkshake into a tall glass, add your choice of decorations or extra fruit and enjoy!

★ PIZZA ★ TIME ★

YOU WILL NEED

* 1 large mixing bowl
* wooden spoon
* tea towel
* rolling pin
* baking paper

Be safe

INGREDIENTS (MAKES 4)

* 300g strong bread flour
* 1 tsp instant yeast (from a sachet or a tub)
* 1 tsp salt
* 1 tbsp olive oil, plus extra for drizzling
* 300g grated cheddar cheese (75g per pizza)
* 1 tube tomato purée
* toppings of your choice

★ TOP ★ TIP ★

Wheat-free pizza! Instead of using pizza dough as a base, use jacket potatoes! Simply bake the potatoes in the oven, cut in half and top as you would the pizza!

TOPPING SUGGESTIONS

Pepperoni, ham, bacon, chicken, sweetcorn, olives, mushrooms, pineapple, peppers, red onion, chilli, spinach....

1. Put the flour into a large mixing bowl and stir in the yeast and salt.

2. Make a hole in the middle of the flour, pour in 200ml warm water and the olive oil. Bring the mixture together with a wooden spoon until you have a 'wet' dough.

3. Lightly flour a work surface. Place the dough in the centre and knead for five minutes.

4. Cover the dough with a tea towel until needed.

5. Split the dough into four even balls and lightly flour a work surface. Roll out the dough into a flat circle with a rolling pin, making sure it is thin.

6. Pre-heat the oven to 240ºC/475ºF/gas mark 7.

7. Place the pizza bases onto baking paper, cover the bases with tomato purée, spreading it to the edges, and top with cheddar cheese.

8. Now it's time to decorate! Add all your favourite toppings or even make some funny faces!

9. Place on the top shelf of the oven (still on the baking paper) for 8–10 minutes. Make sure the base is nice and crispy before serving!

The bush monsters

The bush animals lived in a huge and wonderful place with endless blue skies, trees for shade and huge rocks that glowed red in the sun. Animals were flying, hopping, walking, crawling, slithering and swimming all over the place. But there was one problem. The bush animals were such a mixed bag of shapes and sizes that they kept themselves to themselves.

When the bush animals did cross paths, they exchanged pleasantries, but nothing more. 'Hi Snake,' said Koala when Snake slithered by her shady tree. 'What's up Koala?' replied Snake and slithered on his way. As Koala watched him go, she thought, 'Wow! Snake is so long and footless and shiny and scaly.' And Snake thought, 'Awww. Koala is so grey and soft and cuddly and cute.' And then they shook their heads thinking, 'But we're far too different to ever be friends.'

It was the same story all over the bush. Emu would come to a dusty screeching halt and say 'Alright Platypus?', whenever she spotted him by the watery creek. 'Oh hello Emu,' Platypus would say, while thinking 'Cor! Emu is so fast and big and shaggy-feathered and amusing'. And Emu would shake her head, thinking, 'Platypus is amazing; so duck-billed and flat-footed and sleek.'

From Kangaroo and Kookaburra to Spider, Possum and Crocodile, the bush animals all felt the same: 'We're far too different to ever be friends.' So, they carried on keeping themselves to themselves.

But one day something happened that changed everything.

The bush animals were going about their usual daily business. Snake was curled up on a flat warm rock, Koala was sleeping and Kangaroo was taking her joey down to the creek. Everyone was doing very different things in different places but they all heard the same noise. 'BBBBBRRRRRRRUUUUUUUUUUUUUUUUUUUUUMMMMMMMMMMMMMM!!!'

Kangaroo and Wallaby may have been the only true jumpers, but everyone jumped! Several animals moved to higher ground to see what was happening, some rushing wildly, some crawling nervously, and they eventually gathered on a hill overlooking the bush under Koala's eucalyptus tree. They stared down in amazement at several huge, yellow animals – monsters – that they'd never seen before. 'What are they?' the bush animals exclaimed. 'And what are they doing?'

As if in reply, the yellow monsters roared towards the bush and, slowly, began eating through the trees – chewing branches and leaves and anything else in their path. 'Noooooooooooooooooooo!' shouted the bush animals together, as they watched the giant creatures devour their beloved bush home. Soon, many more bush animals came scuttling and jumping and crawling and flying up the hill to escape from the monsters and join the others under Koala's tree.

All day the monsters ate and ate and ate. Finally, just as the sun was setting, they left in a cloud of dust. The bush animals looked down at the vast empty space where half the bush used to be. 'What are we to do?' they all thought in silence.

The next morning the bush animals gathered under Koala's tree. 'Who are these monsters?' wailed Possum in despair. Kangaroo, who had seen more of the world than most of the bush animals, spoke: 'I think they are beasts of labour, and do the bidding of humans that ride them.' 'Humans, hhmmmmmmm...', the animals murmured. Almost every bush animal knew about humans, but few had ever come across them. Rumour had it that humans were best avoided.

'This is a catastrophe!' said Emu. 'They've already eaten half the bush – what if they come back for more?'

'We have to stop them!' Wombat cried. 'But how? Those yellow monsters are so much bigger than any of us!' Spider pointed out.

'We need a clever plan,' said Bat, and everyone nodded their heads in agreement. And so the bush animals got their heads down together to hatch a clever plan. All day there was arguing and shouting and stamping, and at one point Kookaburra called Platypus 'a weird duck-nosed non-beaver.' In the end though they all agreed and they came up with a plan.

'aah!'

The next morning, as the sun rose higher and higher, the humans and their monsters returned. The bush animals had gathered under Koala's tree again and were waiting – ready to put their plan into action.

They watched the yellow monsters creep up to the edge of the remaining bush then stop. From inside one of the monsters a bald human emerged. It walked back and forth, possibly trying to decide which tree to eat first. Just then Snake jumped out, stretched fully in the air, then coiled himself around the human's neck. 'Arrrrggghhhhh!' screamed the human, shaking Snake off and bolting back into its monster.

The animals cheered, but not for long. The monsters began to roar again and charged towards the bush. 'Phase 2!' shouted Emu, and instantly the nearest monster screeched to a halt. The other monsters stopped as well and, rather cautiously, their humans emerged, looking around to make sure Snake was nowhere in sight. Eagerly they walked up to a tree where Koala and her baby had suddenly appeared. They crowded around Koala and made strange noises like 'Ahhhh!', 'Ooohh!', 'Aaaaw' and 'Sweeeet.' The humans stood around for a long time admiring Koala and her baby, until the bald human, who'd stayed behind in his monster, growled at the others. 'We ain't got time for cute koalas! Back in your trucks all of you – we have work to do!'

Under the tree, the animals groaned. 'Time for phase 3,' signalled Emu. Right on cue, Kookaburra and his friends flew over the humans and started laughing raucously. The humans stopped to look up, and some even laughed along. But then the cackling became louder and louder. Kookaburra and his pals whirled around the humans, who began to panic. 'Arrrgh!!', 'It's hurting my ears!', 'I can't bear it!', 'Make them stop!', yelled the humans. They started to run back to their monsters, but before they could move several sank into the earth up to their waists. Wombat had sneakily dug tunnels underneath, causing the ground to give way and swallow them. 'Good work Kooks and Wombie,' nodded Emu with approval.

Eventually the humans made it back to their monsters, which roared again with their big chopping arms and legs and headed for the bush animals' precious remaining trees. 'They're asking for phase 4,' sighed Emu, 'send the signal to Croc'. Now, no one really wanted to resort to Crocodile, as he could be a bit scary, but they were left with no other choice. Crocodile and his entire clan emerged from the river and slowly crawled towards the monsters. Soon the ground was a moving mass of scaly skin. Meanwhile, Human Bob, the leader, had got out to guide the monsters around Wombat's pits when he suddenly saw the crocs. 'Crocs! Millions of them!' he yelped in terror and dived headlong back into his monster.

The crocodiles were soon face to face with the monsters. Snapping their teeth and lashing their tails Crocodile and his mates began forcing the monsters back. The monsters roared in return but their nervous humans knew that they had to retreat, or risk being surrounded by the crocs.

Up on the hill the rest of the bush animals watched and cheered wildly as the crocodiles drove the monsters away. When the crocodiles returned triumphant, everyone was celebrating and frolicking about with glee. No one could stop talking: 'Kookaburra, your laugh was brilliant!', 'Snake, you were so brave!', 'Crocodile, you were really scary!', 'Koala, I thought they were going to try and steal you, you were so cute!'. They danced around together, jumped for joy and chattered as the sun went down and the stars came up and sparkled in the dark night sky like diamonds.

'Why don't we hang out like this more often?' asked Spider, sitting on Possum's shoulder. 'I dunno,' said Possum, 'I think I just thought I was too furry and big and pink-nosed and brush-tailed to be friends with you.' 'And I thought I was too titchy and eight-legged and fast and scuttly to be friends with you!' Spider replied. 'Isn't it silly?' they said at the same time and laughed. As the bush animals celebrated through the night, and their voices rose up into the sky, there and then it was clear – no longer would they keep themselves to themselves.

the end

TOP 10 baby animals!

Here are ten babies of the wild animal kingdom which we think have the highest cute-factor! What would be your top ten?

1

POLAR BEAR CUB
Polar bears almost always have twins. The cubs are born into warm, cosy dens that their mums have dug specially for their birth.

2

GIRAFFE CALF
Giraffes give birth standing up – that means that the babies fall about 1.5m to the ground when they are born! Despite this, after half an hour they can stand up and after only ten hours they are ready to run with their mums!

3

GIANT PANDA CUB
Panda cubs are surprisingly tiny when they are born. They weigh only about the same as an average-sized tomato!

4

ELEPHANT CALF
Sometimes an elephant calf sucks its trunk, just as a human baby sucks its thumb!

26

5

EMPEROR PENGUIN CHICK

An Emperor penguin chick is first cared for by its dad, sometimes for a couple of months, while its mum goes off to sea to bring back food. And then it's mum's turn to keep the chick warm and snug in the freezing Antarctic weather!

6

BABY MONKEY

A baby monkey is born with a strong grip – much like a human baby in fact! It means it can cling tightly to its mother's fur and hitch a ride around on her back.

8

KOALA (JOEY)

When a koala baby (a joey) is born, it's only about the same size as a jellybean! Straight away, the joey crawls into its mother's pouch, starts to suckle milk and doesn't come out again for about six months!

7

Badge link
Friend to animals
Wildlife explorer

TIGER CUB

Like kittens, tiger cubs are born blind and without teeth. After a week, their eyes open, but their mum looks after them until they are between 18 months and three years old.

10

RED DEER CALF

People sometimes think red deer calves have been abandoned. Not true! Their mums deliberately give birth out of sight from predators in long grass or bracken. Until the calf is strong enough to run with the rest of the herd, it stays hidden and its mum visits it regularly to feed it.

SEAL PUP

Northern fur seal mums and their pups use special calls to speak to each other. Scientists have found that they can recognise each other's calls even after being apart for more than four years!

9

Top Brownie games

KNIVES, FORK AND SPOONS

You need a clear room or an outdoor field to play. Everyone has to line up against a wall or behind an imaginary line. One person is a caller. If she calls out 'lay the table' everyone has to run to the opposite side of the room. If she calls 'clear the table' everyone must run back. If she calls 'knives' everyone must stand to attention. If 'spoons' is called out everyone must crouch down. If 'forks' is called everyone must stand up straight with arms above their head.

SUN AND FROST

This is a very simple game of tag. One player is the sun and another is the frost. Everyone has to run around, and the frost has to catch them. Anyone caught must stand still, until the Sun comes and defrosts them. Change over often so that everyone gets the chance of being Sun and/or Frost.

FIND THE LEADER

Everyone sits in a circle with one person 'it'. 'It' must cover her eyes while someone else is chosen to be the leader. The leader starts an action, like clapping hands, clicking fingers, stamping feet, etc, and the rest must follow. 'It' then opens her eyes and must guess who the leader is. The leader has to keep changing the action. The others must watch the leader out of the corner of their eyes to see what the new action will be. 'It' has three goes to guess who the leader is. If she guesses correctly or runs out of guesses then two new people become 'it' and leader.

Do you think Brownie games are a lot of fun? Why not share some of your favourites with your friends and family? Here are some suggestions.

FRUIT SALAD

A classic! If you don't already know how to play it read on to find out how it goes. Everyone sits in a circle and gets named, in turn, 'apples', 'bananas' and 'pears'. To play the game, a caller stands in the middle and calls out 'apples', 'bananas' or 'pears'. All the players named the fruit called out must get up then run around the circle clockwise and back to their seats. The caller can also shout 'fruit salad', which means EVERYONE has to run around the circle. The last person to sit down is out and must turn around and face the other way. Keep playing until there's just one person left.

MONKEY FOOTBALL

You'll need some balls to play this game – any type will do, footballs, sponge balls, tennis balls, etc. Smaller balls makes the game more difficult. To play, everyone stands in a circle, feet apart and touching with their neighbour's. The space between your leg is the goal, and you must block balls from getting through using your hands and arms. You must also try to score and get others out by rolling the balls through their legs. If a ball gets through your defence you lose the use of one arm. If another gets through you lose both arms.
A third ball means you're out. Play until there's one winner.
Never throw the ball – you may only roll it on the ground.
Anyone throwing a ball gets a red card and is out.

How did you like the games? Can you think of your own favourite? Write it down here.

Badge link

29

Penguin games

Inspired by the Winter Olympics and Paralympics in Vancouver, Canada, the penguins are having their own sporting showdowns!

Illustrated by Gemma Hastilow

FIGURE EIGHT
Trace the lines to see which ice artist has managed a perfect '8' to win this competition.

BELLYSLEIGH
Trace this Emperor daredevil's course safely through the maze!

BIG AIR
Fit the missing jigsaw piece to see who hit the heights!

30

SLALOM

Oh dear, there's been a ski mix-up! Match the pairs correctly.

SKI JUMP

Who says penguins can't fly! Spot the 10 differences

CURLING DRAMA

It's all very tense and down to you, the ref, to decide who came closest!

Bad hair day

Ever wake up with such bad hair you have to wear a hat? Or even stay under your duvet? Does it stick up in all the wrong places and lay flat as a pancake everywhere else? With this activity you can find out just how bad your hair could really look!

1 Find a good-sized photo of yourself and trace the outline of your face onto white paper.

2 Carefully cut out your head shape from the piece of paper with scissors.

Badge link
Artist
Craft

3 Let your imagination run as wild as your hair and draw a wacky hairdo around your face shape. How about a curly blue hair or spiky purple hair? Or what about green hair down to your ankles?

4 Pop your drawing on top of your photo. What a mad hairdo! If you have a camera you could take a photo of your creation to show your friends.

5 Cut out as many head shapes as you like and think of loads of hairdos to try out on your face. How about finding photos of your mum, dad, friends, pet or favourite toy to give them a makeover?

6 If you are feeling artistic why not add a body with some groovy clothes? How about swirly rainbow hotpants or stripy flares and a dotty waistcoat?

Weird science

Science is a lot of fun; you learn new things and it gives you a chance to get messy! Scientists often mix different things together to see what happens. Try these experiments and get some strange and surprising results of your own!

You will need

- a bowl
- 2 heaped tablespoons of cornflour
- 30ml of water
- a couple of drops of food dye (you can make it any colour you like!)

IT CAN BE MESSY, SO WEAR AN APRON!

GOO!

1. Spoon the cornflour into the bowl.
2. Add the water and food dye.
3. Mix it together with your hands until it's blended.
4. Now experiment with the mixture! Take some in your hands and play with it. Try pressing it. What happens? Let it sit in your palm. What happens?

The weird thing about cornflour mixed with water is that the goo you end up with acts like a liquid and a solid. Cornflour is made up of long stringy particles. When you press the goo with your finger, the force, or pressure, from your finger makes the particles join together and feel solid. But if you leave the goo on the table or sitting in your palm, the particles have no pressure on them and slide around loosely like a liquid. WEIRD!

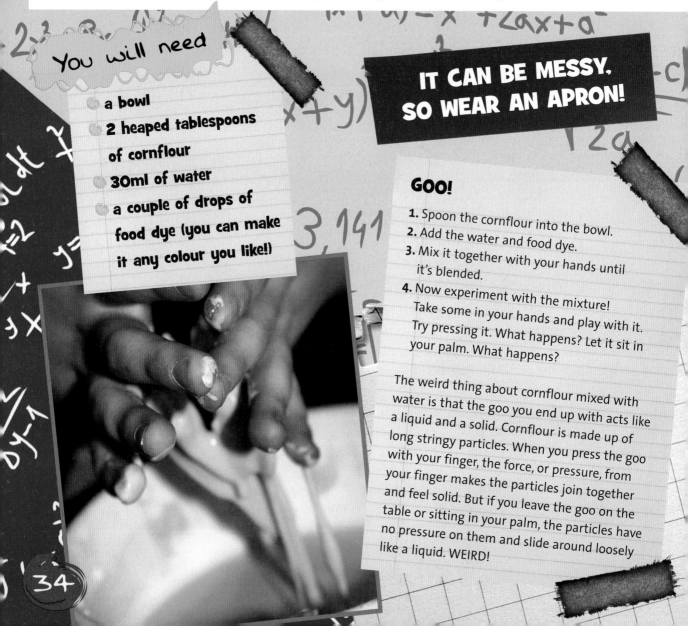

You will need

- a small plastic bottle
- vinegar
- washing-up liquid
- a couple of drops of food dye
- a square of tissue
- a heaped teaspoon of bicarbonate of soda
- an old newspaper

When you mix vinegar and bicarbonate of soda they react together to make a gas called carbon dioxide. Carbon dioxide makes the bubbles you get in fizzy drinks. In the experiment, these carbon dioxide bubbles react with the washing-up liquid and make the foam that spills out of the bottle!

SURPRISE!

1. Half fill the plastic bottle with vinegar.
2. Add the food dye and a squirt of washing-up liquid.
3. Swirl the bottle to mix the liquids.
4. Stand the bottle on top of the newspaper.
5. Carefully tip the teaspoon of bicarbonate of soda into the middle of the tissue. Roll it up and twist the ends.
6. Drop the tissue ball into the bottle.
7. Wait for a minute or two. What happens?

Badge link

Science investigator

You in the frame

Put yourself in this story! Take pictures of yourself and a friend in various poses, then simply insert into the story.

Main characters:
Kita – Lead Brownie
Nina – Best friend
Charlie – Another Brownie
Jo – Leader
Katy – Young Leader

'How are we going to mark this special occasion?'

'Come on Kita,' shouted Kita's mum, 'it's nearly time for Brownies.' Kita was really excited about Brownies this week because she knew her Leader Jo was going to tell everyone about a special party.

At Brownies

'Did you know that Rainbows, Brownies, Guides and Senior Section members – that's Young Leaders like Katy and other girls in guiding aged 14 to 26 – are all going to be 100!' said Jo. Kita liked to go to Brownies and choose what games to play each week, and she really wanted to be a Sixer one day too.

This week Jo wanted to tell the Brownies all about the Centenary celebrations. Guiding was 100 years old this year and that was just fab! 'We are all going to celebrate, won't that be exciting?' said Jo. Kita and the other Brownies were feeling giddy. It was a

crazy idea that everyone was 100 and there were so many ways to celebrate.

'How are we going to mark this special occasion?' asked Jo. All of the Brownies jumped up and shouted. 'Bouncy castle, belly dancing, cake!' screamed the Foxes. 'Horse riding, candy floss, games!' called the Hedgehogs. All the Leaders were giggling – they were pleased because everyone's ideas were very good and imaginative. It was already home time so Jo asked everyone to sit down and listen carefully. 'Ok!' said Jo, 'with so many good ideas, we'll have our work cut out. Next week is half term so there is no Brownie meeting, please use the time to think about how there has been 100 years of guiding and how we could celebrate. Bring your ideas back to Brownies and we'll have a vote to decide the best ones.'

Take a photo or draw a picture of YOUR ideas for celebrating 100 years of guiding.

This was too much for Kita's brain to contain. She was bursting with excitement all the way home. Pop, pop, pop – ideas were popping in Kita's mind. 'We could make a big banner and ask the Mayor to hang it near the shops,' she thought, 'or hold a big party and invite the whole town.' Kita just couldn't stop thinking. Pop, pop, pop.

At the weekend

Kita's dad took her to the park to meet up with her best friend Nina who was also a Brownie, but she went to Brownies on a different day. They loved to spin on the roundabout until they felt too dizzy to walk. 'I'm wobbly,' said Nina, 'let's sit on the swings and talk.' Nina and Kita often talked about what they did at Brownies because sometimes they did extra badges at home together for fun. Kita's thoughts were still popping in her head like popcorn so she decided to tell Nina all about what Jo had said at Brownies and what she was thinking now.

'Cool! I've got it. We should make something special to celebrate being a hundred,' said Kita.
'What do you mean?' asked Nina, 'make what?'
'I don't know, may be a box of all our favourite things,

with pictures and photos. We could write a story about what it is like to be a Brownie.'
'Why would we do that?' Nina looked puzzled.
Kita said 'To bury in the garden silly!'
Now Nina was doubly puzzled.

Kita's brain and mouth worked extra hard telling Nina all about her idea. They could bury a box of things – like the special trinkets they kept in their Promise boxes at Brownies – and bury it in their garden. 'Then, in 2020, 2060 or even the year 2210,' said Kita 'someone would discover it and find out all about us!'

It was an interesting idea. Even Nina knew that.
What do YOU think?
a) *Clever idea* ☐
b) *The best idea anyone has ever had, ever* ☐
c) *Not that great, I've seen something*
   similar before ☐

Little did Kita and Nina realise, but behind the long red slide, just before the park gate, Charlie had been listening very, very carefully to Kita's inspirational idea. Charlie knew Kita because they lived next door to each other; they were also quite good

37

friends at Brownies, although Charlie was a little bit younger. Charlie knew Nina because they went to the same school. Charlie was only seven and wanted to be as clever as the older girls – always thinking and having ideas popping in their heads. Charlie knew that it would be fun to see how Kita and Nina would make their box of 'Brownies in 2010' stuff, and maybe Charlie could copy Kita's idea and make something similar.

At Kita's home the next day

Nina came to Kita's house to start filling a box with photos and pictures. Kita and Nina got straight to work. Kita's mum explained that the special box they were trying to fill and bury in the garden for Brownies of the future to find was known as a time capsule. This made it sound even more exciting.

'What shall we put in the box?' asked Nina.
'Let's show people where we live and what it looks like,' said Kita.

Nina had brought her sister's camera to Kita's house so that they could take photos and print copies of the photos from Kita's computer. It was a lovely sunny day so both girls went into the garden at the front of the house to take a photo.

Take a photo or draw a picture of objects that you would include to represent what it is like to be a Brownie in 2010.

Kita emptied her Promise box and started to fill the time capsule with some of her favourite Brownie trinkets, a badge, some pictures and some sparkly hair bands she liked to use.

When Kita and Nina had filled an old box with lots of things for Brownies of the future to find, they took the box to the garden to decide how and where they were going to bury it.

In the garden

'Let's put the box here and look around the garden for a safe spot to bury it,' said Kita. Nina left the time capsule box on the table next to the fence and thought about what Brownies of the future would look like.

Peeping over the fence, Charlie was secretly watching Kita and Nina as they became more and more serious about burying the time capsule. Charlie really, really wanted to see what was in the box that Kita and Nina had made so that she could make one too. Reaching as far as she could to pick up the time capsule box from the table in Kita's garden, Charlie's face was getting

Take a photo of where YOU live to add to the time capsule too.

What do you think Brownies would look like in the year 2210? Take a photo or draw a picture.

cross and very red. Charlie had another idea. 'I know,' she thought 'I'll stand on this bucket and use this twig on the floor to push the box closer to me so that I can reach it.'

Leaning as much as she could, Charlie finally touched the time capsule box with her twig. Kita and Nina were prodding their fingers in the soil and couldn't see what Charlie was doing. Kita heard some scratching noises behind her and turned around to look.

'Hey!' called Kita. Nina turned around too to see what all the fuss was about. 'What are you doing with that twig?'

Just as Kita had started to shout, Charlie's foot slipped on the bucket and her legs started to wobble. Charlie fell towards the fence and the twig in her hand pushed the time capsule box off the table! All of the photos, drawings and Brownie trinkets that Kita and Nina had collected for the special time capsule fell into the muddy soil.

'Oh no!' whimpered Nina, 'what now?'

Kita knew that Charlie only wanted to look at the time capsule box and didn't mean to make the box fall into the mud. The photos and trinkets were all messy from the muddy soil but would be okay with a bit of water and some care. The drawings were messy forever and would have to be thrown away.

'I'm so sorry,' said Charlie.
'That's ok,' said Kita, 'you didn't mean to do it.'

Pop, pop, pop went Kita's brain. 'I know!' she said, 'I have a better idea – we should make some more drawings with Charlie and then take the time capsule box to Brownies. We can show Jo and Katy and make one big one together!'

'That really was a good idea,' said Nina and Charlie.

THE END
(If you liked this activity have a go at the competition on pages 54–55! Look out also for the 'Catch the Moment' photography competition at www.girlguiding.org.uk/centenary.)

39

2010 Horoscopes

ARIES
(ADVENTUROUS, ACTIVE AND OUTGOING)

Aries girls are outgoing and they love a good adventure! 2010 is definitely your year to get active. You could try a new sport or activity, or maybe make it your New Year's resolution to get your Dancer or Agility badge at Brownies. Whatever you do, make sure you have lots of fun doing it!

21 MARCH – 19 APRIL

CANCER
(FUN, POPULAR AND LIKES TO CHANGE HER MIND)

Cancer girls are the girls everyone wants to be with, but recently you have been changing your mind quite a lot. 2010 is the time to think about something or someone else. Maybe you can help out a younger girl in your Pack or look after an animal? Give your time to someone who needs it and you'll both feel great!

21 JUNE – 22 JULY

TAURUS
(COOL, CALM AND CHILLED OUT)

Taurus, you're as cool as a cucumber! You're also a great listener when your friends need someone to talk to, but make sure that you make some time for yourself too. This is the year to take up a hobby you've always wanted to do, like writing stories or even a bit of yoga – then you'll be even more chilled out in 2010!

20 APRIL – 20 MAY

LEO
(CHEERFUL, STYLISH, GOOD SENSE OF HUMOUR)

Cheerful Leos try not to let anything get them down, and people just love having you around because you're always positive. You have a fab sense of style and you're great at making people around you feel good about themselves. Treat your friends to a makeover and see what wonderful things will happen in 2010!

23 JULY – 22 AUGUST

GEMINI
(CURIOUS, MISCHIEVOUS AND LOVES TO LEARN)

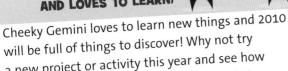
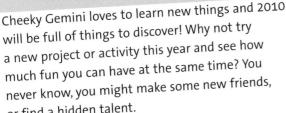

Cheeky Gemini loves to learn new things and 2010 will be full of things to discover! Why not try a new project or activity this year and see how much fun you can have at the same time? You never know, you might make some new friends, or find a hidden talent.

21 MAY – 20 JUNE

VIRGO
(SUCCESSFUL, CREATIVE, CARING AND THOUGHTFUL)

Clever Virgos are great planners because you always think things through carefully. In 2010 put your talents to good use and plan a party for you and all your friends, maybe to celebrate the Centenary! With your caring, sharing nature, the party is certain to be a great success and you could even get your hostess badge while you're at it!

23 AUGUST – 22 SEPTEMBER

What's in store for you and your friends in 2010? Find out now!

LIBRA
(HAPPY-GO-LUCKY, ROMANTIC, BUSINESS-MINDED)

Librans are happy-go-lucky by nature and you take everything in your stride! You've got a good head for business too, and this year the time could be right to plan a fundraiser for a cause close to your heart. It's your opportunity to shine – don't miss it!

23 SEPTEMBER – 23 OCTOBER

CAPRICORN
(QUITE LIKES BEING CHALLENGED, WORKS TOO HARD)

Quiet Capricorn is hard-working and always aims to be the best. You've got a bright future ahead of you, and you want to work hard and do well. But remember that all work and no play makes Capricorn a dull girl. Be sure to take the time this year to have fun with your friends and challenge yourself in a different way.

22 DECEMBER – 19 JANUARY

SCORPIO
(WISE, LOYAL AND STUBBORN)

As the most loyal of all the star signs, Scorpio girls make the best friends. However, be careful not to be too stubborn when you find something or someone you believe in. Know when to let go, and then make the most of your new-found freedom! You might find what you're looking for when you least expect it!

24 OCTOBER – 22 NOVEMBER

AQUARIUS
(GENEROUS, CARES A LOT, INTELLIGENT)

2010 is the age of Aquarius so this really is your year! Aquarian girls are naturally caring and want to change the world around them for the better. Use the extra energy that your star sign gives you this year to get creative. Grab your Brownie friends and start making the world a better place!

20 JANUARY – 19 FEBRUARY

SAGITTARIUS
(A FREE SPIRIT, ADVENTUROUS, OPTIMISTIC)

Sagittarians are free spirits who love to try new things. This year get in touch with your inner explorer and go on an adventure. If the North Pole seems too far away, try an overnight expedition in your local area. Don't forget to involve your Brownie friends; after all, the best part of an adventure is chatting about it afterwards!

23 NOVEMBER – 21 DECEMBER

PISCES
(STRONG, IMAGINATIVE, DAYDREAMER)

As natural leaders, Pisces girls are destined for great things in 2010. But while your head is in the clouds, make sure you keep your feet firmly on the ground! You have a great imagination, so make this your year to show the world what you're made of, turn your dreams into reality and prepare to shine!!

20 FEBRUARY – 20 MARCH

41

Pick of the bunch

Go bananas in the kitchen with these yummy recipes!

BANANA LASSI

A lassi is a very popular thirst-quencher in South Asia. Often it's flavoured with salt, pepper and spices but this is the best version if you've got a sweet tooth.

Ingredients

- 2 ripe bananas, peeled
- 250ml natural yoghurt
- pinch of cardamom powder
- pistachio nuts or flaked almonds, chopped up
- ice cubes

Be safe – nut allergy

 blender tall glass

Badge link

Cook   Cook

1 Put the bananas, yoghurt and cardamom powder in a blender. Whizz until smooth.

2 Find a tall glass and put a couple of ice cubes in the bottom. Pour the lassi over the ice and sprinkle the chopped nuts on top. Drink with a straw!

42

SQUIDGY BANANA FLAPJACKS

You know that black and squishy banana at the bottom of your bag? Well, you don't have to throw it away because old bananas are perfect for baking!

Ingredients:

- 110g butter
- 2 tbsp light brown sugar
- 5 tbsp golden syrup
- 1 ripe banana
- 180g rolled oats

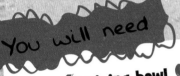
You will need

🍎 mixing bowl 🍎 fork
🍎 large saucepan 🍎 20cm tin

1 Mash up your banana with a fork in a mixing bowl.

2 Heat the butter, sugar and golden syrup in a large saucepan until it's all melted. Stir in the oats and mashed banana and then spread the mixture evenly in the tin.

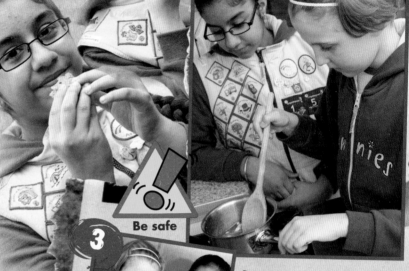

Be safe

3 Bake at 190°C/375°F/gas mark 5 for 15–20 minutes until golden brown. Cut into pieces while it's still warm and then leave it to cool in the tin. Eat them right away or keep them fresh in an airtight box and enjoy a tasty breaktime snack tomorrow!

FAIR BANANA

A lot of farmers in poorer countries rely on the money they get from growing bananas to feed their families, get medicine and send their children to school. Fairtrade companies buy the bananas from farmers at better prices, which means they can do these things. So look out for the Fairtrade sticker in the supermarket when you're buying your bananas!

THE WHOLE BANANA

In many parts of Asia, they use banana flowers, and sometimes even the soft inside of the banana plant trunk, in their cooking. Banana leaves are often used to wrap up or serve food in (it makes the food taste better than plates or paper!) and they make great umbrellas in the monsoon!

TOP BANANA!

Mmmmm, bananas – they're tasty, filling AND good for you! They contain lots of potassium, fibre, protein, vitamins and some very useful minerals too.

43

Marble games

Marbles have been played with for thousands of years. If you find a good partner to play against you can have a fun competition. Many of these games are played outside, but some of the games could be played indoors too.

TYPES OF MARBLES

Look in your local toyshop for marbles in various sizes and lots of pretty colours. Some have colourful swirls, some are milky, and some are just one colour. Different marbles have different names – why not ask your dad (or other grown-up) the funny names he called marbles when he was little?

Badge link

Agility

Hobbies

WHAT DO I DO WITH A MARBLE?

Kneel down and flick your marble so that it goes where you want it and quite quickly! Put your thumb behind your first finger and use your thumb to push that finger to flick the marble. Try not to move your whole hand!

HOLE GAME

Two or more players
For this one you need a small hole in the ground. If you can't find one, ask permission before you dig one or use a flat target. From a starting line flick your marble into the hole. The player with the most marbles in the hole wins.

CHASE GAME

Two players
One player flicks her first marble out. Then, take turns trying to hit the other player's marbles. Pick up each one you hit. The winner is the player with most marbles at the end.

PLAYING FOR KEEPS

You might be happy to let each other keep the marbles you win in your game, but if you are not, say so before you start!

CIRCLE GAME

Two players
Make a circle on the ground with a skipping rope. In the middle use 13 marbles to make a cross. The idea is to knock these marbles out of their cross shape with another marble, from outside the circle. Pick up any marbles you knock from the cross. The winner is the player with most marbles at the end.

Drawing masterpieces!

Badge link

Artist

Create a work of art block by block!

Have you ever wanted to draw something really, really well? Well, here's your chance! Find out just how easy it is to create your own masterpiece!

Simply choose a drawing from the ones below that you want to copy. Then, take your pencil and start copying it onto the drawing area on the right – box by box. And that's it!

If you wish, colour in your finished drawing. Show it around and compare it with what your friends drew.

Feel like drawing some more? Maybe you want to draw ALL of the sketches below? Simple! Just copy or trace the large square diagram on to a spare piece of blank paper then start drawing all over again!

Brownies

Savannah soccer

It's the football World Cup 2010 in South Africa, and all the animals are limbering up for the action!

Illustrated by Gemma Hastilow

BACK OF THE NET!

Find the best route to goal for Lion.

CHEETAH'S CHEERERS

How many animal mates are cheering Winger Cheetah on? Unscramble the words to find out.

POPHI   SICTRHO

HONIR   POLERAD

ZAGLLEE   NEYAH

KERMEAT   DOROCICEL

TRAWE FUFABOL

WHAT A KEEPER!

How many practice balls is Goalie Giraffe trying to save?

SPOT THE DIFFERENCE

Find 10 differences between these two illustrations.

LINE UP

Match the correct shadows to the correct players.

SEEING STRIPES

Can you spot where the ball is?

49

Story gathering

You will need
* Paper
* Pens
* Photographs (optional)

★ BROWNIE ★ FAMILY ★ TREE

Find out which members of your family have been involved with guiding. For example, maybe your mum or aunt was a Brownie once, you might have a cousin who is a Rainbow or perhaps your Dad or Uncle might recall if their mum was a Brown Owl.

Draw a family tree with you at the start. Make links to all the people in your family who have been in guiding. You could add pictures of your family, perhaps old ones of them in their Brownie clothes!

Think about making your tree even bigger and include your friends or neighbours. Now, who would you like to choose from these people to interview about their time in guiding?

★ SHARPEN ★ YOUR ★ INTERVIEW ★ SKILLS

To make a good interviewer, you need to ask interesting questions and listen carefully to the answers. Try playing these games to test how good you are!

Who am I?
Play this game with your friends. Write the names of celebrities or famous people on some sticky labels and place one on each player's back. The game is to work out who you are by asking the other players the right questions. You can ask as many as you like but the answers can only be 'yes' or 'no'. How quickly can you identify who you are?!

Copy cat
Sit back to back with a friend (or friends). Each of you should have matching sets of shapes, such as a square, a triangle, two circles, etc (different-coloured building blocks also work well).

One person starts by building something with her shapes. She must then get the others to do the same without showing, only telling. This can be tricky without looking so think carefully about how to describe each piece. The other person needs to listen very carefully to understand where to place each piece. Did your shapes turn out the same or were some bits different?

Badge link

Brownie traditions

Communicator

Writer

Everyone loves a good story and some of the best tales are those that are based on real people and the things that they have done. To celebrate guiding's Centenary, we are collecting stories from as many people as possible – and we need your help! Try out these activities to find out how!

COMPETITION

If you enjoyed the activities then perhaps you're ready for our competition challenge! Interviewing someone and writing their story takes a variety of skills. You have to be a good listener as well as a bit of a detective to dig out the really interesting stories. Asking good questions helps!

What to do:

1. Ask your parent for permission to take part.

2. Find someone to interview who you think has a great story to tell about guiding.

3. Take along a list of questions you would like to ask about their time in guiding: What did they wear? What were the best activities? Where did they go to camp? What did they learn?

4. Write up your favourite story from your interview and check the details with the person whom you interviewed and make sure they are happy for you to use their story.

5. Email your interview story to centenary@girlguiding.org.uk. Write 'Brownie Annual 2010 Competition' in the subject box. Remember to include your name, your age, your address, your Brownie Pack and the name of the person you interviewed in the email and send it before the closing date of 28 February 2010.

★ The winning entry will be chosen to feature in the 2011 Brownie Annual! Winners will be notified by 1 April 2010. ★

All entries will be featured on our story-gathering website. Visit www.girlguiding.org.uk/centenary to read about what girls have been getting up to over 100 years of guiding!

Web safe

The adventures of Flat Brownie!

Have you heard of Flat Stanley? He is a boy in a story by Jeff Brown who had the good fortune to be flattened by a bulletin board. It's quite an advantage being flat and Stanley went on plenty of adventures as a result.

Imagine what you could do if you were flat? Stanley pretended to be a picture in a gallery once and helped catch sneaky art thieves, he also flew like a kite and went down a drain to find his mum's ring. But Stanley's biggest adventure was when he visited distant friends – his parents put him in an envelope and posted him there! Don't worry, they gave him a sandwich for the trip!

How about sending a Flat Brownie on an adventure? Here's a Brownie for you to cut out and colour in (or trace her and colour her in). Think about some of the fantastic adventures she could go on and write them in a letter to a friend.

Now it gets exciting. Pop your Flat Brownie in an envelope with the letter and put her in the post. Ask your friend to write a letter describing more adventures to send back to you or to send on to other friends.

How far will Flat Brownie get? Maybe all around the world!

If you've enjoyed this why not take a look at www.flatstanleyproject.com and talk to your school teacher about getting involved?

Web safe

R AVION

LETTER-WRITING

Isn't it exciting to get something in the post? Letter-writing is a good way to keep in touch with friends and it's lovely to imagine them reading your letter!

1 Choose some pretty note paper.

2 Put your address on the right-hand side of the page.

3 Underneath and on the left-hand side start your letter with 'Dear...,'

4 Don't forget to sign off with 'Love...,'. Why not decorate your letter with a picture or a pattern?

Badge link

Artist

Communicator

World traveller

Writer

Dear Helen,

This is flat Brownie, please look after her.

She likes cookies and ham sandwiches.

Please pass her on so she can enjoy her adventure!

Love from

Kimberly xxx

Do polar bears get cold?

Questions you've always wanted answered

CUNNING CREATURES

Q: Why do lizards lose their tails?
A: It's a brilliant getaway tactic! If an enemy grabs the lizard by the tail, the tail just breaks off! All the enemy is left with is a wriggling tail!

Q: How do crocodiles brush their teeth?
A: Well, they don't need a toothbrush because they have a bird called a plover to do it for them. The crocodile lets the little bird pick its teeth for scraps of food – the croc gets clean teeth and the plover bird gets a meal, so everyone's happy! No, the crocodile never eats the plover, that would be rude!

Q: Which animal fishes for food?
A: The alligator snapping turtle has a long, bright red piece of skin on its tongue that looks just like a wiggling worm on a fish hook. Fish swim towards it looking for a meal and... SNAP!

Q: Which animal is the cleverest?
A: Chimpanzees are some of the brainiest animals in the world. They even make special tools to help them find food to eat! They rip leaves off a thin stick and poke it into an anthill to get the ants to come out and then gobble them up!

WEIRD BODIES

Q: Do polar bears ever get cold?
A: Never! Quite the opposite, sometimes they get too hot and have to roll around in the snow to cool down! This is because they have a really thick layer of fat under their skin which keeps them warm even when they swim in icy waters.

Q: Which animal has stretchy skin?
A: The sun bear, which lives in Southeast Asia, has very loose skin around its neck. If a tiger, or another predator, grabs it, the bear can turn around in its skin and bite back! Ouch!

WHAT A SIGHT

Q: Are bats really blind?
A: No, not at all. They see perfectly well in daylight. It's just at night time that they can't see as well, just like us!

Q: Do caterpillars need glasses?
A: If they did, they'd need six pairs! Even though most caterpillars have 12 eyes, their eyesight is still really bad. They can only tell the difference between light and dark. Some caterpillars don't even have any eyes. They get around by touch and smell alone.

STRANGE BEHAVIOUR

Q: Why don't I beat my chest like a gorilla?
A: Well, you can if you want to settle an argument, but it might be easier to talk! Two male gorillas will beat their own chests, roar, bark at each other and tear up leaves in an argument. Usually the smaller gorilla will back down so the situation won't end in a fight.

Badge link

Friend to animals

Wildlife explorer

GREEDY GUTS

Q: Which is the greediest animal?
A: Vultures are scavenging birds, which mean they feed mostly on the carcasses (bodies) of dead animals. As many as 100 vultures will swoop down to feast on a carcass and some vultures will eat so much they can't fly afterwards.

Q: What's the strangest thing a shark has eaten?
A: Tiger sharks are known for eating anything and everything. One of the strangest thing on record was a set of bongo drums once found in a tiger shark's stomach!

Q: How many ants does it take to fill up an anteater?
A: A lot! The giant anteater eats up to 30,000 ants a day!

Cupcakery

These ultimate rainbow cupcakes are quick and easy to bake and can be decorated any way you want!

Ingredients (makes 12)

- 160g self-raising flour
- 160g caster sugar
- 160g butter
- 2 large free range eggs
- 5g baking powder
- 3 food colourings (red, blue and yellow)

Be safe

You will need

- 3 mixing bowls
- weighing scales
- electric whisk
- wooden spoon
- cupcake baking tray
- white muffin cases (these are best for bigger cupcakes!)

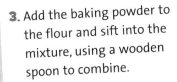

1. Preheat oven to 180° C/350° F/gas mark 4. Mix sugar and butter in a large bowl using an electric whisk (or using wooden spoon) until creamy.

2. Whisk in the eggs, one at a time.

3. Add the baking powder to the flour and sift into the mixture, using a wooden spoon to combine.

4. Split mixture equally into three bowls.

5. Add a few drops of the red food colouring to one of the bowls, mixing well and adding more colouring until you get the shade you want. Repeat with the yellow and blue colourings. Make sure they are very bright!

6. Place the muffin cases in the baking tray. Spoon the yellow mixture into the cases using a teaspoon. Make sure the mixture is even and spreads all the way to the sides, repeat with the blue then red mixture. The cases should be half full after the three layers.

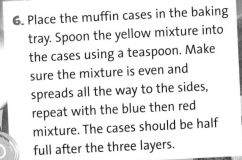

7. Place cupcakes in the oven and cook for 14–18 minutes (until risen). Check regularly!

Badge link

8. When the cupcakes have risen, use a wooden skewer to pierce the centre of one cake. If the skewer is clean when pulled out, the cupcakes are ready!

LET'S DECORATE!

TOPPING FOR 12 CUPCAKES

A. ICING: 85g softened butter and 175g icing sugar. Put the butter in a large mixing bowl and beat well until creamy. Gradually sift in the icing sugar until mixed well. You can add food colourings or flavourings to make the icing more exciting!

B. FROSTING: 200g full fat soft cream cheese, 25g soft butter and 225g icing sugar. Put the cream cheese and butter in a large mixing bowl. Using an electric whisk, beat together until creamy. Sift in the icing sugar and continue to whisk until well mixed. You can also add food colourings to this topping to match your cupcake theme!

C. FLAVOURED ICING: 280g mascarpone cheese, 60g icing sugar, one rind of an orange, 1 teaspoon of lemon juice. Put all the ingredients in a large bowl and beat together until mixed well. Instead of the orange rind and lemon juice you can add other flavours, like vanilla or even a teaspoon of chocolate, strawberry or maple syrup.

D. CHOCOLATE TOPPING: 110g butter, 230g icing sugar, 50g melted plain chocolate. Put the butter in a mixing bowl and beat well until creamy. Sift in the icing sugar and beat together until smooth. Finally add the melted chocolate and beat again until mixed well.

TOP TIP!

Ready-to-roll coloured icing can be bought from the supermarket and is a great way to decorate your cupcakes! Use it to make flowers or animals, or use cookie cutters to make cool shapes and patterns!

61

What a character!

Create your own stories with these characters! For even more fun, get together with friends and create a story together, then perform it!

MIA, 5,

is Amma's little sister. Mia wants to join Rainbows but her Mum has said that she needs to wait until she is older. Mia thinks this is unfair as her friends at her new school are members of the local Rainbows. Mia's favourite thing in the whole world is her pet cat, Whiskers. Mia sometimes fights with her older sister Amma but only when Amma teases her.

AMMA, 8,

has just moved to Little Morton with her Mum and Dad and is looking forward to joining Brownies. She was a member of a unit in her old hometown and misses her friends from the Rabbit Six. Amma's favourite subject at school is English and as well as Brownies she enjoys going to ballet lessons. Amma has a little sister.

GRANDAD DOUG

is Amma and Mia's Grandfather. He has lived in Little Morton all his life but rumour has it that he used to be a spy for the Government and travelled all over the world. Amma loves visiting Grandad Doug and hearing his stories about his adventures.

KAREN

is Amma and Mia's Mum. She moved to Little Morton to be closer to Amma and Mia's grandfather. She likes being back in her old hometown and has started to catch up with old friends already.

PAUL

is Amma and Mia's Dad. He is very busy with his new job, but still enjoys playing football on a Saturday. He is very pleased that Amma likes Brownies and is looking forward to going camping with her when the weather gets better.

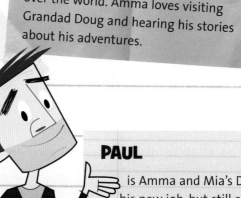

ANGELA

is Amma's Brownie Leader and Karen's best friend from primary school. Angela is pleased that the family has moved back to Little Morton and enjoys spending time with Karen and the rest of the family. Angela also owns the local post office and knows all the gossip in the town.

Badge link

Entertainer

Writer

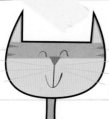

WHISKERS

is Amma and Mia's pet cat. She is a tabby with long whiskers and she enjoys having her tummy stroked – but only when she feels like it! Whiskers is actually very clever and knows exactly when Karen is going to get up in the morning so she can be ready at the bedroom door meowing for her breakfast.

CARLY, 7,

is Amma's best friend from her old primary school. Carly misses Amma now that she has moved away but her Dad has said that she can go to visit her at half-term. Carly is keen to meet Grandad Doug as she wants to be an explorer when she grows up and is interested to hear his stories of travelling around the world.

MINTY, 9,

is in Amma's new class at school. Minty plays the trombone in the local cadet marching band and is really good at maths. Amma quite likes Minty but feels bad about finding a new best friend as she feels she should stay loyal to Carly.

JAMIE, 14,

is Rachel's older brother. He goes to the secondary school in Great Morton and plays guitar with his mates in a band called the 'Crazy Cats'. Sometimes he babysits Amma and Mia, and he has promised to teach Amma how to ride her bike during the summer holidays.

AMY, RACHEL & KEIRA, 8, 8 & 9,

are all at Amma's new school. They are very popular and Amma and Minty are a little bit scared of them. Rachel's older brother is in a band so she tells everyone that she has met loads of famous people. Amma is never sure whether to believe her or not.

ReCYCLE your bike!

Here are some top tips for making your old bicycle something to be proud of again!

JAZZY WHEELS

Make a slit down one side of the straws with a pair of scissors (you will need an adult to help you with this). Clip the straws onto the wheel spokes.

Badge link

Artist

Designer

Cyclist

Road safety

BASKET CASE

Get some multi-coloured pipe cleaners and a small basket. Use three pipe cleaners to attach the basket to the front of your bike between the handlebars. Use more pipe cleaners to decorate the basket by weaving them through.

HOT SEAT

If you cut plastic bags into strips, and then tie them around the seat post, they will look like streamers and blow in the wind as you ride. Make sure the streamers are short enough not to get tangled in the wheels or chain.

NAME THAT RIDE

Why not make some fun, colourful, nameplates out of cardboard and attach them to your bike?

REMEMBER NOT TO LEAVE YOUR NEWLY DECORATED BIKE OUT IN THE RAIN AND MAKE SURE EVERYTHING IS ATTACHED SECURELY!

Guides 100

Guess who's turning 100 years old!

★ MOVING ★ ON

Being a Brownie is great fun – you get to spend time with your friends, try out new things, make cool stuff and visit exciting places. And, of course, one of the best things about being a Brownie is that the adventure doesn't end on your tenth birthday! When you are ten you can join Guides. Guides are girls aged between 10 and 14, and 2010 is a really special year for the Guides because it is their 100th birthday!

★ NO ★ RUNNING! ★ NO ★ JUMPING!

A hundred years ago the world was a very different place. George V, grandfather of HM Queen Elizabeth II, was King of England. Girls still had to wear long skirts and weren't allowed to run in public. Entertainment was different too, for example, even though you could go to the cinema with your friends, the first talking movie would not be shown for another 17 years!

★ BOYS ★ HAVE ★ ALL ★ THE ★ FUN

The Girl Guides started when girls decided that they wanted something for the girls too. A famous army general, Robert Baden-Powell, started the Boy Scout Movement in 1907 and boys all over the country were taking part in this exciting new adventure. A group of girls decided that they also wanted to join in the fun and so they sneaked into the Boy Scout Rally at Crystal Palace in South London in 1909. After pushing their way past 11,000 boys to get to the front of the crowd they asked Baden-Powell if he could start something for the girls.

★ HOW ★ GUIDING ★ BEGAN

Baden-Powell was so impressed by the enthusiasm of this group of girls that he decided to start a whole new adventure just for them called the 'Girl Guides'. In 1910 the Girl Guides Association was formed with Baden-Powell's sister Agnes Baden-Powell in charge.

Badge link

Brownie traditions

World guiding

Culture

★ BADGES ★ BADGES ★ BADGES

Back in 1910 Girl Guides could earn badges for helping in hospitals, electricity repairs and learning semaphore. But the world has changed a lot in the last 100 years and so have the Guides. Today you can take part in Go For It! challenges on all sorts of topics from Chocolate to Football. You can earn badges by learning about anything from circus skills to party planning and best of all you get to do all these things while having a lot of fun with your friends!

Joining Guides means starting a whole new adventure – one that has been going on for 100 years. Ask your Leader how to join in too!

GIRL GUIDES

Wildlife explorer

MUSIC GROUP

COMMUNICATOR

What was that?

What do you think these animals are saying?
Make up your own funny animal captions
to go with each picture.

Wordy challenge

Give your brain a workout with these fiendish riddles.

DINGBAT

Decode the words or phrases hidden below.

Eyed / eyed	jumpppppppp	L L I H
Legged Legged Legged race	O*range*	finger
TOE	a t b u o	Daddy l l e e g g g g g g

ICE-CREAM SUNDAE

A	R	X	F	U	D	G	E	B	M
H	V	A	N	I	L	L	A	I	A
D	I	E	S	B	A	S	N	E	J
P	J	U	S	P	L	T	I	T	V
S	T	R	A	W	B	E	R	R	Y
E	O	K	G	B	D	E	M	B	L
L	F	A	E	A	P	R	R	O	Z
C	F	G	I	N	G	E	R	R	N
V	E	Z	P	A	I	B	X	S	Y
P	E	C	A	N	Y	E	A	T	N
L	C	K	C	A	R	A	M	E	L

Find these yummy ice-cream flavours hidden in the grid.

- Vanilla
- Raspberry
- Mint
- Strawberry
- Toffee
- Pecan
- Banana
- Caramel
- Lemon
- Fudge
- Ginger

When you've found them all, tick off all the remaining letters that appear more than once. There'll be six letters left. Unscramble these to find out how you WOULDN'T feel if you had a scoopful of all these flavours for your pudding!

PICTURE POSTCARD

You get a letter in the post and it's no ordinary letter! Can you work out who sent it and what it says? Try writing a reply in the same way!

 R U? hope U R It was + 2 C U at Brow last week.

 8 all the    we made in the car on the  home.

Except for 1 which saved for m pet w . W

did do with yours? Do U w to come over xt

 day? will w again m s .

Love from h m  y.

WHO AM I?

Are you a bookworm? Find out! Write the answer to each clue in the grid below. Hint: the last letter of one answer is the first letter of the next. If you write out the letters in the red squares in order below you'll find another famous character.

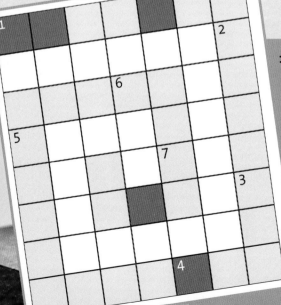

1. She's the smartest girl in school with a special way with a wand.

2. As an elephant, he is unusually colourful!

3. _ _ _ _ _ Dahl

4. Jacqueline Wilson's twins Ruby and Garnet are definitely a

_ _ _ _ _ _   _ _ _

5. The Billy Goats Gruff came across a particularly ugly one when crossing a bridge.

6. She makes a dangerous voyage to the Arctic North in search of her friend Roger and her father, Lord Asriel.

7. She walked through a looking glass!

Mystery character: _ _ _ _ _

 71

Ballerina puppet show

Staging your very own puppet show is as easy as one, two, three!

ONE – MAKE THE PUPPETS

1 Cut the tip of the toe off an old stocking and tie a knot 10cm down from the top.

You will need

- cardboard tubes
- bendy straws
- cotton wool
- sticky tape & string
- pens
- paintbrushes
- garden cane
- old stockings/tights
- thin strips of fabric
- buttons
- paint
- glue

2 Stuff some cotton wool into the stocking down to the knot and tie it off. This will be the head of the ballerina.

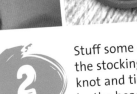

3 Thread the long bit of stocking down a cardboard tube then tape down tightly on the inside at the other end.

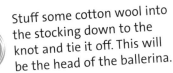

4 Paint and decorate your cardboard tube so that it looks like a ballerina – you may want to use thin strips of fabric to make a ballerina skirt, which is called a tutu.

5 Cut two 20cm lengths of string and attach to the bottom of the tube as legs. Attach a large button to the end of each leg – these are the feet.

6 Cut two 10cm lengths of string and attach them to the sides of the tube as arms. Attach a large button to end of each arm to act as hands.

7 Stick a length of garden cane onto the back of the cardboard tube so you can hold the puppet. On each arm button attach the shorter end of a straw with sticky tape. (When you use your puppet, you will be able to bend the ends of the straws and hold them to move the ballerina's arms and legs so it looks like she is dancing.)

8 Cut the top of the stocking above the head into strips to look like hair and draw on the face.

Make as many ballerinas as you like. You could even make a ballet teacher!

TWO - TO THE THEATRE

Use large cardboard boxes to make a puppet theatre and decorate as shown.

Badge link

Artist

Craft

Toymaker

Dancer

Entertainer

THREE - ON WITH THE SHOW!

With your friends controlling a puppet each, enact this little show. Remember to leave one Brownie free to be the narrator (the person who reads the story out).

There were two Brownies named Esmay and Sarah
Working on their Dancer badge together
They started ballet and then found out
This hobby they simply couldn't be without!

They had so much fun pirouetting around
Leaping and gliding, their feet off the ground
But after a while a small problem arose
A little dilemma in the hobby they chose.

While talented Sarah looked set to go far
Showing potential of becoming a star
Poor Esmay wasn't doing so well during practice
And their teacher Miss Humphries was beginning to notice.

She said she thought that it would be best
If Sarah alone went on with the rest
Advising Esmay to sit out and look
To pick up some tips from Sarah's book.

But Sarah and Esmay were such good friends
Sarah realised this unfairness would have to end
So she said to her teacher 'I'm having fun
But my friendship means more so I'm declaring I'm done!'

Now, her teacher managed to persuade her to stay
And said 'how about some fun for you and Esmay.
For the final part of your badge you know
You have to put on a small dance show!'

So Esmay and Sarah danced together
Because Brownie friends are friends forever!

74

If you liked this little tale, why not create your own story too?

Brownie shopping

There are lots of special gifts available to celebrate 100 years of guiding – here's just a few of them!

Brownies teddy clips
7859 **£2.60**
Height: 7.5cm.
Age 3+.

Brownies Centenary bear
7854 **£5**
Height: 15cm.
Age 3+.

Hoodie-style notepad
Notepad with stylish 'section wear' cover. Replacement notepads are available so this fantastic cover gets extra-long use!
9x13cm.
7848 **£3**

Scrunchies
7895 **£3**
Perfect for keeping your hair tidy and also the officially approved way of securing your Centenary neckerchief!
Pack of three assorted colours.
65% polyester, 35% cotton.

Rubber ducks
7869 **£3**
Net of three rubber ducks.

Brownie scrapbook accessory set
7875 **£5**
Brownie-themed accessories for your scrapbook set. Contents may vary.

Pencil
7840 **35p**

Monopoly

7882 **£26**

An exciting new edition of the best-selling board game Monopoly™, specially commissioned for Girlguiding UK. Progress through the guiding sections, visiting favourite guiding places, making your fortune!

The Girlguiding UK edition features the trademark Monopoly money and counters, but also has special guiding touches: the Community Chest has become Community Action and there are new guiding versions of some of the Chance cards. Landing on the wrong square will still land you in jail, however!
Age 8+

 **Girlguiding UK** Trading Service

Three easy ways to shop

 At our depots & shops
Ring 0161 941 2237
to find your nearest one

 www.girlguidingukshop.co.uk
Shop online day or night

for all your guiding wear, books and gifts

 guiding essentials catalogue
Phone 0161 941 2237
Fax 0161 941 6326

Answers

How did you do with all the puzzles? Find out!

WHERE'S ALICE? (PAGES 14–15)
She's next to the Face painting tent. Did you spot her?

PENGUIN GAMES (PAGES 30–31)

Figure eight
Penguin A is the winner!

Bellysleigh

Big air
F is the missing piece.

Slalom
The correct pairs are:
1&3, 2&12, 4&9, 5&6, 7&10, 8&11

Ski jump

Curling drama
Stone 4 is the winning one!

76

SAVANNAH SOCCER (PAGES 48-49)

Cheetah's Cheerers are: Hippo, Rhino, Gazelle, Meerkat, Water Buffalo, Ostrich, Leopard, Hyena and Crocodile.

What a keeper
There are 22 footballs in total.

Back of the net

Seeing stripes

Spot the difference

Line up
Did you match: 1c, 2a, 3d, 4e and 5b?

WORDY CHALLENGE (PAGES 70-71)

Dingbat
Did you get:
cross-eyed, long jump, uphill, three-legged race, orange squash, little finger, big toe, roundabout, daddy-long-legs?

Ice-cream sundae

Mystery word: Hungry

Picture postcard
If you decoded the postcard successfully, it should read:

*How are you? I hope you are well. It was great to see you at Brownies last week. I ate all the fairy cup cakes we made in the car on the way home. Except for one which I saved for my pet weasel. What did you do with yours? Do you want to come over next Friday?
I will write again soon.
Love from Milly.*

Who am I?

Mystery character: Heidi